D1243112

FEDERAL FORCES

CAREERS AS
FEDERAL AGENTS

A CAREER AS A
CIA AGENT

Daniel R. Faust

PowerKiDS
press.

New York

Published in 2016 by The Rosen Publishing Group, Inc.
29 East 21st Street, New York, NY 10010

First Edition

Editor: Caitlin McAneney
Book Design: Mickey Harmon

Photo Credits: Cover (image) Fuse/Getty Images; cover (logo) Color Symphony/Shutterstock.com; cover, pp. 1, 3–32 (mesh texture) Eky Studio/Shutterstock.com; p. 5 (man) Milkovasa/Shutterstock.com; p. 5 (explosion) Vasiliy Smirnov/Shutterstock.com; p. 7 Everett Historical/Shutterstock.com; p. 9 CIA Museum/Wikimedia Commons; p. 10 Robert R. McElroy/Archive Photos/Getty Images; p. 11 The Washington Post/Getty Images; p. 13 Felix Lipov/Shutterstock.com; p. 15 Martin Allinger/ Shutterstock.com; p. 17 (building) AR Pictures/Shutterstock.com; p. 17 (woman) Bevan Goldswain/ Shutterstock.com; p. 19 (main) Ivan Cholakov/Shutterstock.com; p. 19 (control room) ChameleonsEye/ Shutterstock.com; p. 19 (satellite) puchan/Shutterstock.com; p. 21 SAUL LOEB/AFP/Getty Images; p. 23 (main) hxdyl/Shutterstock.com; p. 23 (woman) leungchopan/Shutterstock.com; p. 25 Photo Researchers/Science Source/Getty Images; p. 26 (both) courtesy of the Central Intelligence Agency; p. 26 (coin) courtesy of the Central Intelligence Agency; p. 27 Svajcr/Wikimedia Commons; p. 29 Tyler Olsen/Shutterstock.com; p. 30 tamir shapira/Shutterstock.com.

Library of Congress Cataloging-in-Publication Data

Faust, Daniel R.
 A career as a CIA agent / by Daniel R. Faust.
p. cm. — (Federal forces: careers as federal agents)
Includes index.
ISBN 978-1-4994-1056-3 (pbk.)
ISBN 978-1-4994-1093-8 (6 pack)
ISBN 978-1-4994-1111-9 (library binding)
1. United States. Central Intelligence Agency — Vocational guidance — Juvenile literature. 2. United States. Central Intelligence Agency — Officials and employees — Juvenile literature. 3. Intelligence officers — United States — Vocational guidance — Juvenile literature. 4. Intelligence service — United States — Juvenile literature. I. Faust, Daniel R. II. Title.
UB251.U5 F38 2016
327.12730023—d23

Manufactured in the United States of America

CPSIA Compliance Information: Batch #WS15PK: For Further Information contact Rosen Publishing, New York, New York at 1-800-237-9932

Contents

Spies in Real Life

We've all seen spies in movies and on television. These spies usually drive expensive cars and have exciting spy tools. Do real spies exist? They do, and American spies are part of the CIA, or Central Intelligence Agency. Real spies may be different from the spies we see in movies, but their lives are no less exciting.

The men and women who work for the CIA are highly educated and skilled. They all bring special talents to their job. The CIA employs people with many different backgrounds, including scientists, engineers, accountants, and masters of computers and finance. The agency brings together people who are experts in their field. No matter what their background is, people who work for the CIA have the same goal—to protect the United States and its citizens.

Spies in the movies do exciting things like outrunning fiery blasts and climbing down the sides of buildings. Real spies, like those who work for the CIA, work best when they go unnoticed. Many work undercover, or with secret identities.

The History of Spies

Spying, also called espionage, has been around for thousands of years. Early governments used spies to gather intelligence—or secret information about their enemies—in ancient Egypt, China, Rome, and Greece. Ninjas worked as Japanese spies as early as the 1400s.

America used spies even before the United States officially existed. The American Revolution was a war between England and its American colonies. Patriots, or colonists who wanted independence from England, used spies and other undercover agents against the more powerful and better-organized British army. In 1790, President George Washington asked Congress to create a "secret service fund." The United States government has employed spies ever since. During the American Civil War, both the Northern and Southern states used spies to gather information, capture important mail and documents, and **sabotage** their enemy.

James Armistead

During the American Revolution, George Washington gave Major Benjamin Tallmadge the title of director of military intelligence. Tallmadge created a spy ring in New York City, which was controlled by the British army. This network of spies, known as the Culper Spy Ring, worked in New York City for five years. Tallmadge created a system where numbers were used instead of names. For example, George Washington was referred to as 711. Because of Tallmadge's code, no spy was ever identified.

Born a slave, James Armistead was one of the many spies who worked for the patriots during the American Revolution. Armistead spied on the British army headquarters and camps, gaining important information for the patriots.

Becoming the CIA

On December 7, 1941, the Japanese attacked an American navy base in Pearl Harbor, Hawaii. After the attack, President Franklin D. Roosevelt created the Office of Strategic Services, or OSS. The OSS supplied the United States and its **allies** with military intelligence during World War II. After the war, the OSS was shut down. Its duties were transferred to the U.S. Departments of State and War.

In the late 1940s, political and military unrest began between the United States and the Soviet Union in what is known as the Cold War. The U.S. government needed a central source of intelligence. The National Security Act of 1947 created the Central Intelligence Agency to collect, **analyze**, and deliver intelligence important to the country's security, or safety.

If you're interested in a career in the CIA, it's important to know its history. The CIA Museum in Langley, Virginia, has a lot of information about the CIA's history.

Headquarters

For most of its history, the CIA headquarters in Langley, Virginia, had no official name. It was usually referred to as "Langley" based only on its location. In 1999, the compound, or group of buildings, was officially named the George Bush Center for Intelligence. Former president George H. W. Bush had been the Director of the Central Intelligence Agency from 1976 to 1977.

George H. W. Bush

Because of the need for secrecy, the George Bush Center for Intelligence is a secured area. That means no one is allowed to enter without the proper **authorization**. The center houses offices and agents needed to support the CIA's operations around the world. It's also home to the CIA Museum. This museum contains objects that show the history of the CIA, OSS, and foreign intelligence agencies.

This is the CIA Memorial Wall at CIA headquarters. Each of the 111 stars represents one of the CIA officers who lost their life in service to the United States.

IN HONOR OF THOSE MEMBERS
OF THE CENTRAL INTELLIGENCE AGENCY
WHO GAVE THEIR LIVES IN THE SERVICE OF THEIR COUNTRY

Important CIA Operations

Most of the work the CIA does is never revealed to the public. However, some well-known CIA operations were revealed to the public after they were completed.

In 1979, the CIA teamed up with the Canadian government to rescue six American **diplomats** who were stuck in Tehran, Iran, after the Iranian government collapsed. The diplomats hid for nearly 12 weeks. To reach the diplomats, CIA agents disguised themselves as a film crew making a movie in Iran. The disguised agents were able to help the diplomats escape. This CIA mission became known as the "Canadian Caper."

Operation Neptune Spear was the CIA-led operation that ended in the death of **al-Qaeda** founder Osama bin Laden. The CIA gathered the necessary intelligence, including photographs, about bin Laden's compound in Pakistan.

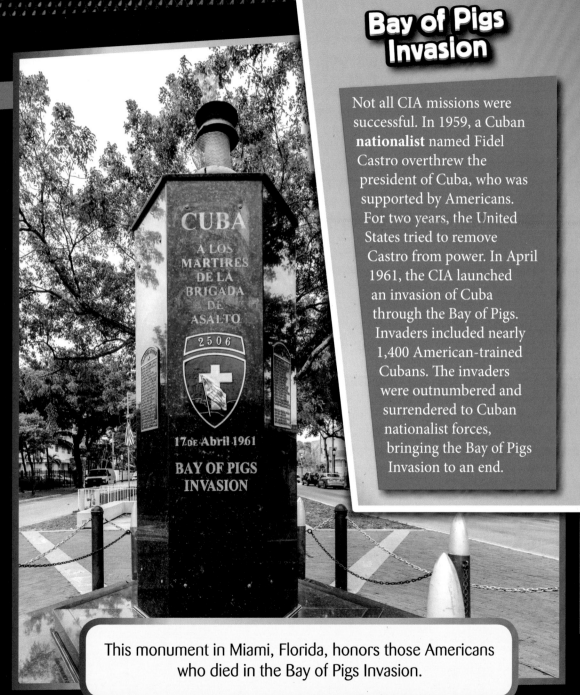

Bay of Pigs Invasion

Not all CIA missions were successful. In 1959, a Cuban **nationalist** named Fidel Castro overthrew the president of Cuba, who was supported by Americans. For two years, the United States tried to remove Castro from power. In April 1961, the CIA launched an invasion of Cuba through the Bay of Pigs. Invaders included nearly 1,400 American-trained Cubans. The invaders were outnumbered and surrendered to Cuban nationalist forces, bringing the Bay of Pigs Invasion to an end.

CUBA

A LOS MARTIRES DE LA BRIGADA DE ASALTO

2506

17 DE Abril 1961

BAY OF PIGS INVASION

This monument in Miami, Florida, honors those Americans who died in the Bay of Pigs Invasion.

What Does the CIA Do?

The main job of the CIA is to gather information about foreign threats. The intelligence is meant to help government and military leaders protect the United States. The information can help leaders make policies on dealing with certain countries or keeping citizens safe in our own country. The CIA also engages in **counterintelligence**, which includes stopping our enemies from gaining secrets and spreading wrong information to confuse them.

The U.S. CIA is divided into four different teams, or directorates. Each directorate has its own area of **expertise**. The National Clandestine Service (NCS) and the Directorate of Science and Technology (DS&T) collect intelligence. The Directorate of Intelligence (DI) analyzes the intelligence and writes reports about it. The Directorate of Support (DS) makes sure the entire process runs smoothly.

The Intelligence Cycle

Step 1: Planning and Direction
CIA agents decide what they'll do and how they'll do it.

Step 2: Collection
Collect information openly (example: watching a foreign news show) and secretly (example: using a hidden camera).

Step 3: Processing
A report is written based on the information collected.

Step 4: Analysis and Production
The information is closely studied and possible outcomes are discussed.

Step 5: Sharing Information
The final written report is given to a political or military leader.

Today, the CIA uses the newest computer technology to send and collect information, while making sure our information is protected from hackers and cybercriminals. Hackers are people who steal information from other people's computers.

Collecting Information

The National Clandestine Service (NCS) is the division of the CIA that deals with collecting intelligence and performing **covert** actions. People who work for the NCS work in countries all over the world. These agents are most like the spies you see in movies and on television.

Officers working for the NCS collect human intelligence, or HUMINT. HUMINT is information gathered through personal contact with human sources. People who are sources of information for the CIA are often called assets.

NCS agents are also responsible for covert actions. Covert actions are missions that attempt to secretly influence the politics, economy, or military of a foreign country. Covert actions are performed when the U.S. government doesn't want its plans or actions to be publicly known.

NCS agents often have covers, or fake jobs and identities, so others don't know they work for the CIA. An official cover involves being posted to a government agency, like a U.S. **embassy**. A nonofficial cover involves pretending to work in a normal job, such as business.

Using Science and Technology

Like the officers who work for the NCS, the officers in the Directorate of Science and Technology (DS&T) also collect intelligence. However, unlike the NCS, the DS&T doesn't collect information from people. These officers rely on audio and video surveillance, or recordings, to collect important information. Audio surveillance includes sound recordings.

Officers who work for the DS&T come from many different backgrounds. They can be computer programmers, scientists, engineers, and analysts. They work closely with the military, experts on certain subjects, and private companies to research and develop the latest technologies that will help keep the United States and its allies safe.

The officers of the DS&T work closely with officers in the NCS, providing technological support to officers around the world.

drone

control room

spy satellite

Officers working for the DS&T often gather intelligence
using spy satellites and drones, like the MQ-1 Predator
drone pictured above. Drones are unmanned aircraft that
carry cameras and other **sensors** to collect information.
Satellites collect information from space.

Creating Intelligence Reports

What happens to all the intelligence gathered by the NCS and the DS&T? This is where the Directorate of Intelligence (DI) comes in. The men and women who work for the DI take the massive amount of information collected in the field, analyze it, and create reports that are read by politicians and military leaders. Even the president of the United States reads reports from the DI.

The DI is divided into 13 different offices. Each office in the DI has its own focus. Some of the offices are concerned with a particular country, such as Iraq, or region, such as Latin America. Other offices deal with global issues, such as drugs, weapons, or terrorism. Terrorism is the use of violence for political aims. This is an important focus for the DI.

Supporting Agents

Spies in movies may look like they travel and work alone on a mission in a foreign country. However, in real life, this isn't the case. In fact, the CIA has an entire department focused on providing backup and support for agents on their missions, or "in the field." The officers of the Directorate of Support (DS) assist agents around the world with everything from security to business-related matters.

The DS is responsible for building and operating CIA facilities, sending necessary equipment, and providing security for agents. This department is also responsible for the CIA's finances and businesses. Medical staff make sure officers are healthy and safe. The DS hires and trains everyone who works for the CIA.

The DS is responsible for organizing transportation for CIA agents. This is important, especially because some agents travel all over the world.

Tradecraft

How do you plant a listening device so it won't be found? How do you follow someone without being seen? Tradecraft is the different **techniques** used in modern espionage. Examples of tradecraft include cryptography and dead drops. These are both important skills for a CIA agent to have. Agents in training have to learn tradecraft in order to gain and analyze information.

Cryptography is the study and practice of codes and code breaking. Codes have been used for thousands of years as a way to deliver sensitive information. Breaking an opponent's codes means you can gain information they don't want you to have. Modern cryptography is also used as a way to protect computer passwords and personal information from cybercriminals.

Dear Friend,
This is a very nice
country. Received your mess...
country. The people are f...
Need assistance of Agent...
and apparently happy.
to carry out instruct...
weather has been very...
operations Monday...
a little rain now and...
Will keep you...
Wish you were here.
Ag...
Your 7...

Tradecraft Terms

CIA agents need to know all the correct terms for tradecraft to carry out missions. A "black bag job" means secretly entering a home or office to steal or copy information. A "dead drop" is a secret location where important items can be left to be picked up by another person. A "legend" is a spy's fake background or biography. A spy's legend is usually supported by documents and memorized details. A "mole" is an agent of one organization sent to work undercover in another organization.

Steganography is the act of concealing a hidden message within another message. In the past, secret messages were written in invisible ink between the lines of an ordinary letter. Today, a digital message or file is sometimes hidden within other digital messages or files.

Real-World Spy Tools

Hollywood spies always have the best gadgets, or tools. While real spies may not use jetpacks or laser-shooting watches, they have used some pretty interesting gadgets over the years. Many devices used by CIA officers are simply smaller forms of ordinary items, such as cameras or binoculars. Making things smaller makes them easier to conceal. Other gadgets are disguised as ordinary objects, such as coins or jewelry.

Other real-life spy gadgets include coins that could hold secret documents, cuff links that contained hidden compasses, and a pipe that received radio signals.

Perhaps one of the strangest pieces of spy gear was the pigeon camera. In 1907, a German inventor named Julius Neubronner strapped a camera to one of his carrier pigeons to track it. Several decades later, the CIA invented a lightweight, battery-powered camera that could be strapped to a pigeon to take pictures as it flew.

Getting a Job with the CIA

Working at the CIA can be exciting and rewarding. The CIA hires people from many different fields. They look for experts in each subject, from economics to technology. The CIA looks for people with excellent communication skills, particularly in speaking and writing. Since the CIA operates all over the world, knowing multiple languages can help you land the job.

Each directorate has certain skills and experience they expect from people they hire. In general, the CIA wants to hire college graduates who have high grades and experience in their field. Most agents have to be willing to move to Washington, D.C., and travel around the world. All employees must first undergo a background check to make sure they've steered clear of crime and drugs. They must also be U.S. citizens.

If you think you may want to work for the CIA, start by studying and staying out of trouble. In a few years, you may be able to get an internship, or a job that pays in experience. The CIA offers internships for high school and college students in a number of different fields.

Why Work for the CIA?

The Central Intelligence Agency provides an important service to the United States. Without the work CIA agents do every day, it would be difficult for our leaders to make the right decisions. The people who work for the CIA are part of a mission to keep U.S. citizens safe.

A career at the CIA is great for an enthusiastic, hardworking person who doesn't mind a challenge. If you like computers, you might be interested in the DS&T. If you like analyzing information, you might like the DI. If you love traveling and using high-tech gadgets, becoming a spy with the NCS would be a perfect fit. CIA agents work together as a superteam to protect our nation and keep its citizens safe.

Glossary

ally: One of two or more people or groups who work together.

al-Qaeda: A militant Islamist organization that engages in terrorist actions throughout the world.

analyze: To study something deeply in order to find out more about it.

authorization: Permission or approval to do something.

counterintelligence: Activity meant to hide the truth from an enemy or to keep an enemy from learning secret information.

covert: Secret or hidden.

diplomat: A person who is skilled at talks between nations.

embassy: The building where representatives from one country live and work in another country.

expertise: Special skill or knowledge.

nationalist: A member of a political group that wants to form a separate or independent nation.

sabotage: The act of destroying or damaging something on purpose in order to interfere with the actions or plans of another person or government.

sensor: A device that senses heat, light, motion, or sound.

technique: A particular skill or ability that someone uses to perform a job.

Index

Websites

Due to the changing nature of Internet links, PowerKids Press has developed an online list of websites related to the subject of this book. This site is updated regularly. Please use this link to access the list: www.powerkidslinks.com/fed/cia